There, one day, he heard a voice, and presently after was surprised by
the appearance of a mermaid
From "The Yellow Dwarf"
THE FAIRY BOOK; THE BEST POPULAR FAIRY STORIES
SELECTED AND RENDERED ANEW

Goble's Fairy Tale Illustrations

86 FULL-COLOR PLATES

Warwick Goble

SELECTED AND EDITED BY
Jeff A. Menges

Dover Publications, Inc.
Mineola, New York

Bibliographical Note

This Dover edition, first published in 2008, is an original compilation of illustrations from the following works: *The Water-Babies; A Fairy Tale for a Land-Baby,* Charles Kingsley (Macmillan and Co., Limited, London, 1909); *Green Willow and Other Japanese Fairy Tales,* Grace James (Macmillan and Co., Limited, London, 1910); *Stories from the Pentamerone,* Giambattista Basile, selected and edited by E. F. Strange (Macmillan and Co., Limited, London, 1911); *Folk-Tales of Bengal,* Rev. Lal Behari Day (Macmillan and Co., Limited, London, 1912); *The Fairy Book; The Best Popular Fairy Stories Selected and Rendered Anew,* Dinah Mulock Craik (Macmillan and Co., Limited, London, 1913); and *The Book of Fairy Poetry,* Dora Owen (ed.) (Longmans, Green and Co., London, 1920).

Library of Congress Cataloging-in-Publication Data

Goble, Warwick.
Goble's fairy tale illustrations : 86 full-color plates / selected and edited by
 Jeff A. Menges.
    p. cm.
   ISBN-13: 978-0-486-46521-0
   ISBN-10: 0-486-46521-7
   1. Goble, Warwick—Themes, motives. 2. Fairy tales—Illustrations.
 I. Menges, Jeff A. II. Title.

NC978.5.G63M46 2008
741.6'4—dc22

                                                            2008006613

Manufactured in the United States of America
Dover Publications, Inc., 31 East 2nd Street, Mineola, N.Y. 11501

Introduction

THE GOLDEN AGE of children's book illustration began in the latter half of the nineteenth century, peaking in the decade preceding World War I and ending at the start of World War II. Many factors contributed to the success of children's books during that time—industrial and technological improvements that allowed for great advances in printing; a desire to preserve national heritage at a time of political upheaval; and a willing public that possessed a better education than ever before. In an age before the motion picture became the primary form of entertainment for the masses, publishing was the dominant source of news, teaching, and escape from everyday concerns.

Many Golden Age illustrators, such as Arthur Rackham, Kate Greenaway, Edmund Dulac, Kay Nielsen, and Walter Crane, enjoyed great success. With the boom in the publication of books, newspapers, and magazines, there was an abundance of opportunities in the field; some artists returned to print repeatedly with works that the public would clamor for, much in the same way that a Hollywood star commands film audiences today. And just as the early film studios had movie stars under contract, the publishers sought out the best talents to produce their finest books. British publishing house William Heinemann kept Arthur Rackham busy for most of his career, while competitor Hodder and Stoughton made Edmund Dulac their "leading man." In competing with these two publishing giants, Macmillan and Company of London hired an artist who was a veteran illustrator in the magazines of the day and had already achieved one of his most important commissions, the first release of H. G. Wells's science-fiction masterwork, *The War of the Worlds*, in 1897: Warwick Goble. In 1909 Macmillan Company hired Goble to become their resident illustrator of gift books. Leading up to World War I, and immediately afterward, Goble produced a steady stream of books illustrating tales from the best-known stories of the Brothers Grimm, to exotic tales of the East—all presenting brilliant and memorable images.

Warwick Goble was born in 1862 in London. After attending the City of London School and the Westminster School of Art, he became a successful illustrator with a strength in watercolor. He was already in his late forties when Macmillan commissioned his first large volume, Charles Kingsley's *The Water Babies*. This work today is viewed as one of best editions of the now-classic children's tale, and its publication launched Macmillan successfully into the gift-book market. Goble's second effort for Macmillan, Grace James's *Green Willow* and *Other Japanese Fairy Tales*, led to additional titles featuring an Eastern influence, something that Goble—like Edmund Dulac—became known for.

During World War I, Goble served his country from the drawing office at Woolwich Arsenal. Due to the war effort, paper production was greatly reduced, and the publishing industry never returned to the heyday it had experienced before the war; nevertheless, Goble worked with Macmillan to produce one more large volume, *The Book of Fairy Poetry*, which appeared in 1920.

The three volumes mentioned here, as well as several others that Goble produced for Macmillan—*Stories from the Pentamerone* (1911), *Folk-Tales of Bengal* (1912), and *The Fairy Book; The Best Popular Fairy Stories Selected and Rendered Anew* (1913)—provide the richly diverse source material for *Goble's Fairy Tale Illustrations*. These works were created while Goble was producing his most noteworthy color work. In his late sixties, after a long and successful career, he left illustration for more leisurely pursuits. Warwick Goble died in 1943.

JEFF A. MENGES

February 2008

For Julia

List of Plates

The Plates

Play by me, bathe in me, mother and child
THE WATER-BABIES; A FAIRY TALE FOR A LAND-BABY

Plate 1

She was the Queen of them all
THE WATER-BABIES; A FAIRY TALE FOR A LAND-BABY

Plate 2

From which great trout rushed out on Tom

THE WATER-BABIES; A FAIRY TALE FOR A LAND-BABY

Plate 3

He watched the moonlight on the rippling river
<small>THE WATER-BABIES; A FAIRY TALE FOR A LAND-BABY</small>

Plate 4

We float out our life in the mid-ocean, with the warm sunshine above our heads

THE WATER-BABIES; A FAIRY TALE FOR A LAND-BABY

Plate 5

The fairies came flying in at the window and brought her such a pretty pair of wings
THE WATER-BABIES; A FAIRY TALE FOR A LAND-BABY

Plate 6

He crept away among the rocks, and got to the cabinet, and behold! It was open
THE WATER-BABIES; A FAIRY TALE FOR A LAND-BABY

Plate 7

The most beautiful bird of paradise
THE WATER-BABIES; A FAIRY TALE FOR A LAND-BABY

Plate 8

He saw the fairies come up from below, and carry baby and cradle gently down in their soft arms
THE WATER-BABIES; A FAIRY TALE FOR A LAND-BABY

Plate 9

Pandora and her box
THE WATER-BABIES; A FAIRY TALE FOR A LAND-BABY

Plate 10

From "The Moon Maiden"
GREEN WILLOW AND OTHER JAPANESE FAIRY TALES

Plate II

From "Green Willow"
GREEN WILLOW AND OTHER JAPANESE FAIRY TALES

Plate 12

From "The Star Lovers"
GREEN WILLOW AND OTHER JAPANESE FAIRY TALES

Plate 13

From "Horaizan"
GREEN WILLOW AND OTHER JAPANESE FAIRY TALES

Plate 14

From "The Story of Susa, the Impetuous, I"
GREEN WILLOW AND OTHER JAPANESE FAIRY TALES

Plate 15

From "Flower of the Peony"
GREEN WILLOW AND OTHER JAPANESE FAIRY TALES

Plate 16

From "The Maiden of Unai"
GREEN WILLOW AND OTHER JAPANESE FAIRY TALES

Plate 17

From "The Singing Bird of Heaven"
GREEN WILLOW AND OTHER JAPANESE FAIRY TALES

Plate 18

From "The Fire Quest"
GREEN WILLOW AND OTHER JAPANESE FAIRY TALES

Plate 19

From "The Espousal of the Rat's Daughter"
GREEN WILLOW AND OTHER JAPANESE FAIRY TALES

Plate 20

From "The Strange Story of the Golden Comb"
GREEN WILLOW AND OTHER JAPANESE FAIRY TALES

Plate 21

From "The Jelly-Fish takes a Journey"
GREEN WILLOW AND OTHER JAPANESE FAIRY TALES

Plate 22

Plate 23

From "Urashima"
GREEN WILLOW AND OTHER JAPANESE FAIRY TALES

Plate 23

From "Tamamo, the Fox Maiden"
GREEN WILLOW AND OTHER JAPANESE FAIRY TALES

Plate 24

The Princess as the Ogre's Bride
From "The Flea"
STORIES FROM THE PENTAMERONE

Plate 25

The Lizard showing Goat-Face the Palace
From "Goat-Face"
STORIES FROM THE PENTAMERONE

Plate 26

Grannonia and the Fox
From "The Serpent"
STORIES FROM THE PENTAMERONE

Plate 27

The Royal Proclamation
From "The Booby"
Stories from the Pentamerone

Plate 28

Rita riding on the Dolphin
From "The Three Enchanted Princes"
STORIES FROM THE PENTAMERONE

Plate 29

Marziella on the Sea-shore
From "The Two Cakes"
STORIES FROM THE PENTAMERONE

Plate 30

Cianna and her Brothers
From "The Seven Doves"
STORIES FROM THE PENTAMERONE

Plate 31

Lise, in the Snow, with the Casket
From "The Months"
<small>STORIES FROM THE PENTAMERONE</small>

Plate 32

The King and the Falcon outside the Palace
From "Sun, Moon, and Talia"
STORIES FROM THE PENTAMERONE

Plate 33

Nennillo and Nennella in the Wood
From "Nennillo and Nennella"
STORIES FROM THE PENTAMERONE

Plate 34

She rushed out of the palace . . . and came to the upper world
From "Phakir Chand"
FOLK-TALES OF BENGAL

Plate 35

She took up the jewel in her hand, left the palace,
and successfully reached the upper world
From "Phakir Chand"
FOLK-TALES OF BENGAL

Plate 36

The Suo queen went to the door with a handful of rice
From "Life's Secret"
FOLK-TALES OF BENGAL

Plate 37

In a trice she woke up, sat up in her bed, and eyeing the stranger, inquired who he was

From "The Story of the Rakshasas"

FOLK-TALES OF BENGAL

Plate 38

"You would adorn the palace of the mightiest sovereign"
From "The Origin of Opium"
FOLK-TALES OF BENGAL

Plate 39

He saw a beautiful woman coming out of the palace
From "Strike but Hear"
FOLK-TALES OF BENGAL

Plate 40

"Husband, take up all this large quantity of gold and these precious stones"
From "Strike but Hear"
Folk-Tales of Bengal

Plate 41

At dawn he used to cull flowers in the forest
From "The Man Who Wished to be Perfect"
FOLK-TALES OF BENGAL

Plate 42

The lady, king, and hiraman all reached the king's capital safe and sound
From "The Story of a Hiraman"
FOLK-TALES OF BENGAL

Plate 43

"What princess ever puts only one ruby in her hair?"
From "The Origin of Rubies"
FOLK-TALES OF BENGAL

Plate 44

Coming up to the surface they climbed into the boat
From "The Origin of Rubies"
FOLK-TALES OF BENGAL

Plate 45

The jackal . . . opened his bundle of betel-leaves, put some into his mouth, and began chewing them
From "The Match-Making Jackal"
FOLK-TALES OF BENGAL

Plate 46

A bright light, like that of the moon, was seen shining on his forehead
From "The Boy with the Moon on his Forehead"
FOLK-TALES OF BENGAL

Plate 47

"Is it very far from hence?" asked the wolf. . . .
From "Little Red-Riding-Hood"
THE FAIRY BOOK; THE BEST POPULAR FAIRY STORIES
SELECTED AND RENDERED ANEW

Plate 48

A young girl of wonderful beauty lay asleep on an embroidered bed
From "The Sleeping Beauty in the Wood"
THE FAIRY BOOK; THE BEST POPULAR FAIRY STORIES
SELECTED AND RENDERED ANEW

Plate 49

The only remnant of her past magnificence being one of her little glass slippers
From "Cinderella; or The Little Glass Slipper"
THE FAIRY BOOK; THE BEST POPULAR FAIRY STORIES
SELECTED AND RENDERED ANEW

Plate 50

When the cock had now crowed for the third time, . . . the little men stole down
and disappeared
From "Adventures of John Dietrich"
THE FAIRY BOOK; THE BEST POPULAR FAIRY STORIES
SELECTED AND RENDERED ANEW

Plate 51

At last she remembered her dream, rushed to the grass-plot, and there saw him lying apparently dead

From "Beauty and the Beast"

THE FAIRY BOOK; THE BEST POPULAR FAIRY STORIES
SELECTED AND RENDERED ANEW

Plate 52

The butterfly took wing, and mounted into the air
with little Tom on his back
From "Tom Thumb"
THE FAIRY BOOK; THE BEST POPULAR FAIRY STORIES
SELECTED AND RENDERED ANEW

Plate 53

"Are you not sometimes called Rumpelstilzchen?"
From "Rumpelstilzchen"
THE FAIRY BOOK; THE BEST POPULAR FAIRY STORIES
SELECTED AND RENDERED ANEW

Plate 54

The lady then gave him a purse
From "Fortunatus"
THE FAIRY BOOK; THE BEST POPULAR FAIRY STORIES
SELECTED AND RENDERED ANEW

Plate 55

Riquet with the Tuft appeared in her eyes the most
elegant young man she had ever seen
From "Riquet with the Tuft"
THE FAIRY BOOK; THE BEST POPULAR FAIRY STORIES
SELECTED AND RENDERED ANEW

Plate 56

So at night, when all were asleep, he led the trembling Aslog
over the snow and ice-fields away to the mountains
From "House Island"
THE FAIRY BOOK; THE BEST POPULAR FAIRY STORIES
SELECTED AND RENDERED ANEW

Plate 57

Jack . . . seized the hen, and ran off with her, . . . reached
the top of the bean-stalk, which he descended in safety
From "Jack and the Bean-Stalk"
THE FAIRY BOOK; THE BEST POPULAR FAIRY STORIES
SELECTED AND RENDERED ANEW

Plate 58

At evening-tide she climbed up into a little tree, and purposed
spending the night there, for fear of the wild beasts
From "The Iron Stove"
THE FAIRY BOOK; THE BEST POPULAR FAIRY STORIES
SELECTED AND RENDERED ANEW

Plate 59

"Madam," said he, "since I have had the honour to serve you,
I know not any other happiness that I can wish for"
From "The Invisible Prince"
THE FAIRY BOOK; THE BEST POPULAR FAIRY STORIES
SELECTED AND RENDERED ANEW

Plate 60

These beasts of prey were instantly turned into three little lambs
From "The Woodcutter's Daughter"
THE FAIRY BOOK; THE BEST POPULAR FAIRY STORIES
SELECTED AND RENDERED ANEW

Plate 61

The king took the beautiful maiden on his own horse and conducted her to his castle
From "Brother and Sister"

THE FAIRY BOOK; THE BEST POPULAR FAIRY STORIES
SELECTED AND RENDERED ANEW

Plate 62

"You have but to give me a sack, and a pair of boots such as gentlemen wear
when they go shooting"
From "Puss in Boots"
THE FAIRY BOOK; THE BEST POPULAR FAIRY STORIES
SELECTED AND RENDERED ANEW

Plate 63

Avenant delivered up his phial; the owl flew with it into the grotto,
and in less than half-an-hour reappeared, bringing it quite full and well corked
From "The Fair One with Golden Locks"
THE FAIRY BOOK; THE BEST POPULAR FAIRY STORIES
SELECTED AND RENDERED ANEW

Plate 64

The fairy there welcomed her majesty
From "The Butterfly"
THE FAIRY BOOK; THE BEST POPULAR FAIRY STORIES
SELECTED AND RENDERED ANEW

Plate 65

The king's daughter was overjoyed when she beheld her pretty plaything again,
picked it up, and ran away with it
From "The Frog-Prince"
THE FAIRY BOOK; THE BEST POPULAR FAIRY STORIES
SELECTED AND RENDERED ANEW

Plate 66

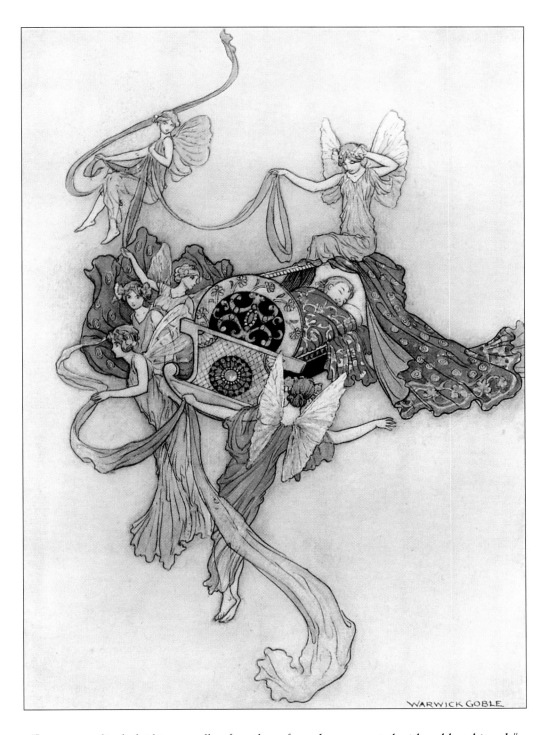

"I was accordingly laid in a cradle of mother-of-pearl, ornamented with gold and jewels"
From "The White Cat"
THE FAIRY BOOK; THE BEST POPULAR FAIRY STORIES
SELECTED AND RENDERED ANEW

Plate 67

He flew in, perched on her shoulder, and expressed his delight and affection by a thousand caresses
From "Prince Cherry"
THE FAIRY BOOK; THE BEST POPULAR FAIRY STORIES
SELECTED AND RENDERED ANEW

Plate 68

They were very friendly, however, and inquired her name. "Snowdrop," answered she
From "Little Snowdrop"
THE FAIRY BOOK; THE BEST POPULAR FAIRY STORIES
SELECTED AND RENDERED ANEW

Plate 69

Stopping beside a fountain, she let her hair fall loose,
and dipped her weary feet in the cool water
From "The Blue Bird"
THE FAIRY BOOK; THE BEST POPULAR FAIRY STORIES
SELECTED AND RENDERED ANEW

Plate 70

The queen threw one of the shirts over each of them,
and when the shirts touched their bodies, they were changed
into swans, and flew away over the wood
From "The Six Swans"
THE FAIRY BOOK; THE BEST POPULAR FAIRY STORIES
SELECTED AND RENDERED ANEW

Plate 71

By the care of the Fairy Tulip, she was not wounded
From "The Hind of the Forest"
THE FAIRY BOOK; THE BEST POPULAR FAIRY STORIES
SELECTED AND RENDERED ANEW

Plate72

And, sweetly singing round about thy bed,
Strew all their blessings on thy sleeping head
From "Good Luck befriend thee"
John Milton
THE BOOK OF FAIRY POETRY

Plate 73

The dun deer wooed with manner bland,
And cowered beneath her lily hand
From "Kilmeny"
James Hogg
THE BOOK OF FAIRY POETRY

Plate 74

Down to the rocks where the serpents creep
From "The Kelpie of Corrievreckan"
Charles Mackay
THE BOOK OF FAIRY POETRY

Plate 75

Buy from us with a golden curl
From "Goblin Market"
Christina Rossetti
THE BOOK OF FAIRY POETRY

Plate 76

**Three spirits mad with joy Come dashing down
on a tall wayside flower**
From "A Fairy Revel, before the coming of Guinevere"
Alfred Tennyson
THE BOOK OF FAIRY POETRY

Plate 77

Oh! they do get away down under the ground,
In hollow pleazen where they can't be found . . .
From "The Veairies"
William Barnes
THE BOOK OF FAIRY POETRY

Plate 78

Instead of crust a peacock pie
From "The Three Beggars"
Walter de la Mare
THE BOOK OF FAIRY POETRY

Plate 79

Sea-nymphs hourly ring his knell: Hark! now I hear them,—ding-dong, bell
From "Ariel's Songs"
The Tempest
William Shakespeare
THE BOOK OF FAIRY POETRY

Plate 80

Wake, when some vile thing is near
A Midsummer Night's Dream
William Shakespeare
THE BOOK OF FAIRY POETRY

Plate 81

For the Nautilus is my boat
In which I over the waters float
From "Fairies on the Sea-Shore"
L. E. Landon
THE BOOK OF FAIRY POETRY

Plate 82

WARWICK GOBLE

And I should look like a fountain of gold
From "The Mermaid"
Alfred Tennyson
THE BOOK OF FAIRY POETRY

Plate 83

What form she pleased each thing would take
That e'er she did behold
From "Lirope the Bright"
Michael Drayton
THE BOOK OF FAIRY POETRY

Plate 84

And the padding feet of many gnomes a-coming!
From "Goblin Feet"
J. R. R. Tolkien
THE BOOK OF FAIRY POETRY

Plate 85